Welcome to your wonderful
Chinese New Year activity book!

Inside you will find everything you need to enjoy
the magic of Chinese New Year and keep you busy
for hours. Have fun with mazes and memory games,
design your own lanterns, and doodle your own dragons.

Discover the story of the Chinese Zodiac and how
the Jade Emperor gave each animal its own year.

Now press out the stencils from the cover and get creative.

Use the super stickers to decorate your doodles
and drawings throughout this book.
Gung Hey Fat Choy! Happy New Year!

Long ago, when the Jade Emperor made the calendar,
he had to decide which animals should rule the years. He invited
all the animals to come to his palace. "Whoever gets here first,"
he said, "will have the honor of ruling the first year."

Of course, all the animals wanted to be first.
So they gathered together and got ready to race.

The animals had to cross a river to get to the palace.
Rat could not swim well, so he asked Ox to carry him
across on his back. When they were almost at the bank,
Rat jumped off and arrived at the palace first.

"You are clever and bold, Rat," said the Emperor. "I will give you the first year. Ox, you are kind and strong, and you shall have the second year."

Next came Tiger. "You are powerful and courageous," said the Emperor. "You shall have the third year."

Rabbit crossed the river by hopping across stones.
"Well done, Rabbit!" said the Emperor.
"You shall have the fourth year!"

Just then, Dragon came
swooping down.

"Dragon!" said the Emperor.
"Since you can fly, I thought
you would get here first!"

"I would have, Your Imperial Majesty," said Dragon. "But on the way, I saw some farmers who needed help. I stopped to make rain for them so their crops could grow."

"That was a noble deed, Dragon," said the Emperor. "You shall have the fifth year."

Suddenly there was a loud neigh, and Horse came galloping through the water. Just as he reached the riverbank, Snake slithered ahead — he had been wrapped around one of Horse's legs!

"Snake, you got here before Horse,"
said the Emperor,
"so you shall have the sixth year.
And Horse shall have the seventh."

A moment later a raft arrived,
carrying Goat, Monkey, and Rooster.
Rooster had found the raft, and Goat
and Monkey had helped him row
it across the river.

The Emperor was pleased that
they had helped each other,
and gave Goat the eighth year,
Monkey the ninth year, and
Rooster the tenth year.

Last of all, Dog and Pig arrived.
"Dog, you are a good swimmer," said the Emperor.
"You should have been here sooner."
"I know," said Dog. "But I was having too much
fun playing in the water!"

"And what made you late, Pig?" asked the Emperor. "I was hungry," Pig explained, "so I stopped to eat. Then I fell asleep!" The Emperor laughed. "You got here in the end, and that is what matters," he said.

"Dog shall have the eleventh year," said the Emperor, "and Pig shall have the twelfth. Now all the years have their rulers. Every twelve years the cycle will begin again. Gung Hey Fat Choy! Happy New Year, everyone!"

Chinese Zodiac

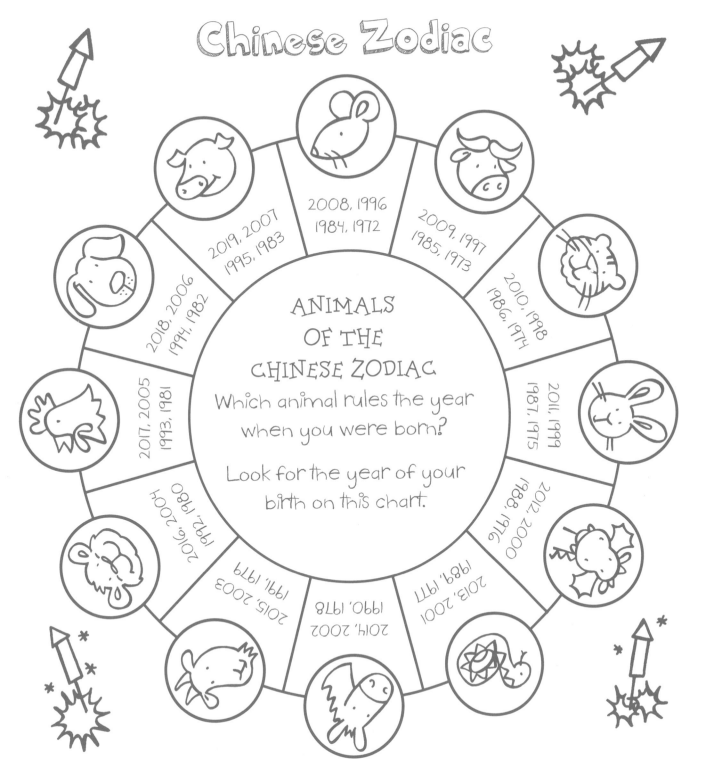

Draw your Chinese year animal

Look at the Chinese Zodiac on the previous page to find the animal of your birth year.

Draw the animal here and color your picture.

Chinese Characters

Trace over the dots to draw the Chinese characters for GOOD LUCK.

Now color them red, the color of good luck!

How to make a lantern

1. Fold a piece of thin cardboard in half.

2. Cut straight lines through the folded edge and stop before the end.

3. Unfold. Bend the card into a cylinder and stick together.

4. Squish.

5. Cut a strip of paper and glue to top edge to make a handle.

Dragon Parade

Lead the dragon parade through town, visiting each
pagoda before arriving at the fireworks.
Color each pagoda when you arrive there.

NEW YEAR CARD

Decorate the border of this Chinese New Year card.

NEW CLOTHES for NEW YEAR

Many people buy new clothes to start the new year.

Color these new clothes.

Color the dragon

Add flames from its mouth
and smoke from its nostrils.

DUMPLINGS!

Dumplings are a favorite food to enjoy
at Chinese New Year meals.

Count the dumplings in each bowl.
Draw lines to connect the bowls that have the same number.

Find the matching lanterns

Now color them all.

WHICH ANIMAL?

Connect the dots to see which animal the Jade Emperor is welcoming.

Which animal is missing?

Read the story to remind yourself and draw in the missing animal.

HELP RABBIT HOP!

Help Rabbit hop across the river by showing him which stones will lead to the Jade Emperor.

DECORATE THE BANNERS!

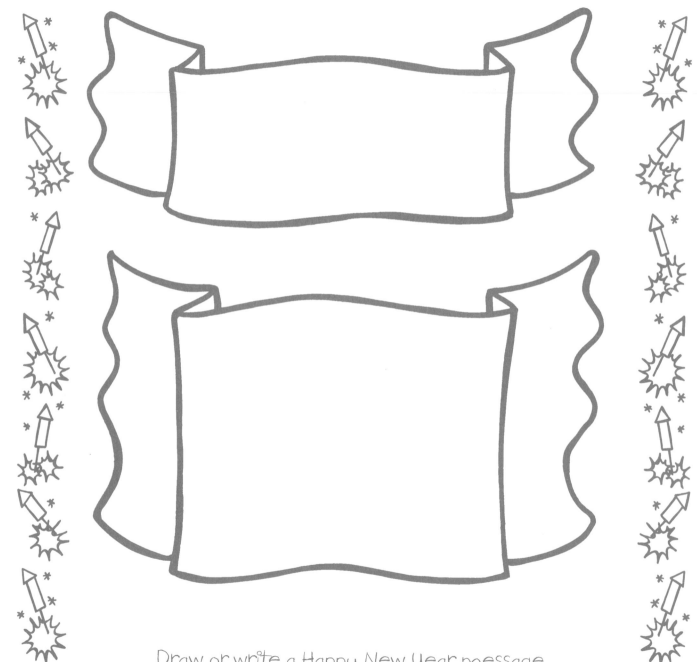

Draw or write a Happy New Year message.

Which puzzle piece is missing in this scene?

1

2

3

4

5

6

BANG THE DRUM!

Chinese people bang drums and gongs to scare away evil spirits at the New Year.

Decorate these drums.

Which Year?

Write the year the Emperor gave to each of these animals.

. . . .

. . . .

Tip: read the story to find the answer.

How to draw a pagoda

Follow these steps to draw a perfect pagoda every time!

RED ENVELOPES

Which envelope has the most money?

Write the number of coins on each envelope.

LANTERN
PAPER CHAIN

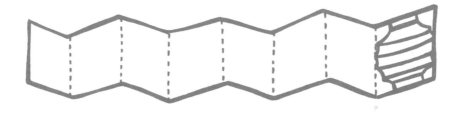

Trace the lantern onto
the front of the folded paper
and carefully cut it out.

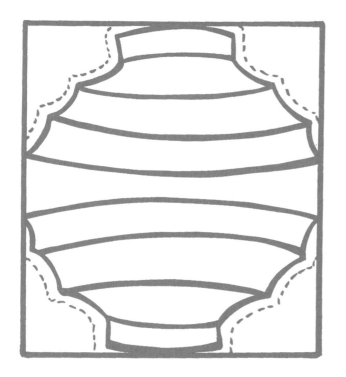

Now open it up and color
your lanterns.

COPY THE PICTURE

Copy the top picture square by square
into the grid below.

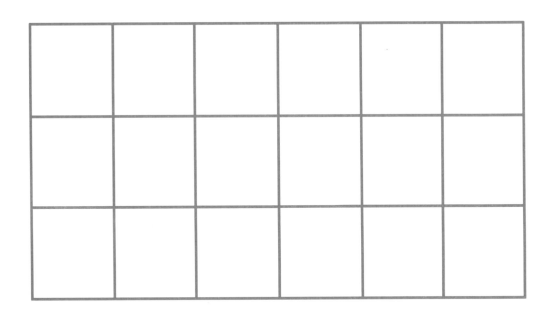

FLOWERS AND FRUIT

Many people visit friends and family to celebrate Chinese New Year, and often bring gifts of flowers and fruit.

Draw some flowers in the vase and some fruit in the bowl.

Memory Game

Look carefully at each picture on this page for 3 seconds.
Then cover up the page and see if you can remember each picture.

COLOR BY NUMBERS

1. Red
2. Yellow
3. Green
4. Blue

Color the lanterns

Tangled Strings

Untangle the strings to see which child gets which red envelope.

THE MOON

The Chinese calendar is a LUNAR calendar, which means it follows the phases of the moon. The New Year festival lasts fifteen days, from the New Moon on day 1 to the Full Moon on day 15.

Draw a round, full moon in the night sky and color the picture.

YOUR PARTY!

Draw pictures of the friends you would invite to your special New Year party, and write their names under their pictures.

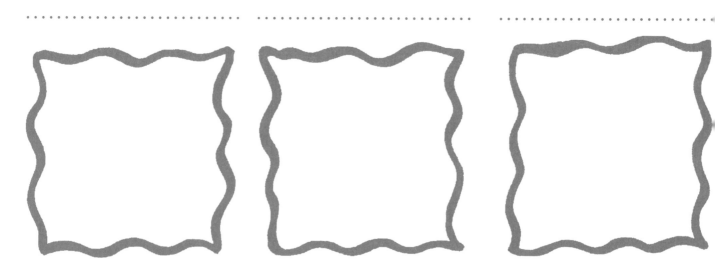

Color the Chinese Lion

Chinese New Year Quiz

1. How many animals raced to the Jade Emperor's palace?

....

2. Which animal got to the palace first?

....

3. How do we say "Happy New Year" in Chinese?

....

4. Which animal had the fifth year?

....

5. What goes into red envelopes at Chinese New Year?

....

Answer: 1. 12, 2. Rat 3. Gung Hey Fat Choy 4. Dragon 5. Coins

FIREWORKS!

Chinese New Year is celebrated with firework displays.

Color this picture and add lots of sparkly fireworks.

How to draw a Chinese lantern

Follow these steps to draw a perfect lantern every time!